8+

Teachers, THAT means LAUGH OUT LOUD.
YUP, science can be HILARIOUS!

LOL Physical Science

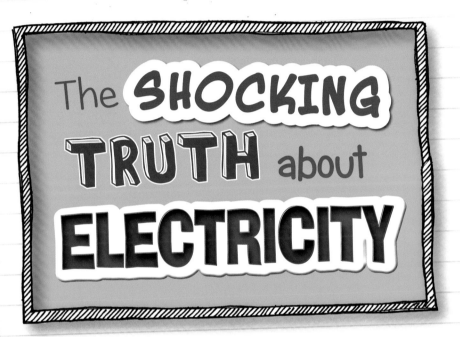

The **SHOCKING** TRUTH about **ELECTRICITY**

by Jennifer Swanson
illustrated by Bernice Lum

Out of the 1,423,950 Jennifers in
the United States, this one likes
science the most.

OK, we can't prove THAT. But SHE
likes science a lot!

Al is a super smart science guy.
He was SHOCKED by HOW awesome
THIS book on electricity is.

Consultant:
Alec Bodzin
Associate Professor of Science Education
Lehigh University
Bethlehem, Pennsylvania

CAPSTONE PRESS
a capstone imprint

Fact Finders are published by Capstone Press,
1710 Roe Crest Drive, North Mankato, Minnesota 56003.
www.capstonepub.com

Library of Congress Cataloging-in-Publication Data
Swanson, Jennifer.
 The shocking truth about electricity / by Jennifer Swanson ; illustrated by
Bernice Lum.
  p. cm.—(Fact finders. LOL physical science)
 Includes bibliographical references and index.
 Summary: "Describes what electricity is and how it works through humor and core
science content"—Provided by publisher.
 ISBN 978-1-4296-8602-0 (library binding) — ISBN 978-1-4296-9300-4 (paperback)
 ISBN 978-1-62065-241-1 (ebook pdf)
 1. Electricity—Juvenile literature. I. Lum, Bernice, ill. II. Title.
 QC527.2.S934 2013
 537—dc23   2011051565

Editorial Credits
Jennifer Besel, editor; Tracy Davies McCabe, designer; Svetlana Zhurkin, media
    researcher; Laura Manthe, production specialist

Photo Credits
Capstone Press: Juliette Peters, 22–23; Corbis: Reuters/Marcos Brindicci, 29 (top);
Dreamstime: Boris15, 6, Dannyphoto80, 13 (right), Gualtiero Boffi, 29 (middle),
John Takai, 13 (left), Lorenzo Rossi, 27 (back); iStockphoto: fotolinchen, 29
(bottom), John Teate, 26, Stacey Walker (frame), cover and throughout; Shutterstock:
baldyrgan (battery), 18, 19, Danny Smythe, 16, Ellas Design, 8, Hywit Dimyadi, 20
(left), iDesign (background), cover and throughout, illusionstudio (poster), cover,
7, iQoncept (one way sign), 18, ittipon, 9 (back), mart (pencil scribbles), cover and
throughout, Miguel Angel Salinas (lightning), 4, montego, 21, Naci Yavuz (road sign),
18, 19, NLshop, 4, Olga Tropinina (arrows and speech bubbles), cover and throughout,
ProfyArt (light bulb), 19, Skyline (notebook sheet), cover and throughout, Tatiana
Popova, 20 (right), tuulijumala (explosion), 3 and throughout, yuri4u80, 10 (right)

Printed in the United States of America in North Mankato, Minnesota.
032012   006672BANGF12

TABLE of CONTENTS

A Hero for All

Electricity is everywhere you look. You can find it in nature, lighting up a stormy sky. It's in your home, making your refrigerator run. And it's in you, making your heart pound and your brain think. Electricity does it all.

This tiny **turbocharged** SUPERHERO can move through wires, walls, and even the World Wide Web. Its mighty power keeps the world safe from darkness and spiders. Simply imagine a world with no phones, no cars, and no lights. And you understand why we call on electricity.

So next time you fail a test, blame it on an electrical malfunction.

Get it? World Wide Web? It's just a joke. Electricity doesn't really battle spiders.

It's a play off the Bat-signal thing.

The joke's not really funny if we have to explain it, is it?

4

So where does electricity's superpowers come from? Turn the page to discover the shocking truth about electricity.

Chapter 1

Charged

To understand electricity, you have to start with the atom. Atoms are extremely small bits of matter that make up an object. You can't see them, but atoms are everywhere. Trucks, countertops, and even your eyeballs are made of atoms. ←

Mind-blowing, right?!?

Every atom is made up of particles. The nucleus is the atom's core. Protons and neutrons sit inside the core. Electrons spin around the core. Sometimes electrons stay very close to the core. But other times, they are more daring and spin far away from it.

Electrons are like little sisters. Sometimes they stay close to Mom. But usually they are running around like little crazy people, getting into everybody else's way, messing with all my stuff, interrupting my friends ... Sorry, got carried away.

WANTED

★ ★ ★ ★ ★ ★ ★ ★ ★ ★ ★ ★ ★ ★ ★

TWO ATOMIC PARTICLES ARE WANTED IN
ATOM. APPROACH CAREFULLY. THEY ARE
CHARGED AND DANGEROUS.

JESSE "THE ELECTRON"
JAMES

BABY FACE PROTON

ONE OTHER PARTICLE IS
KNOWN TO ASSOCIATE
WITH THESE OUTLAWS.
HE IS NOT CHARGED,
BUT IS CLOSELY LINKED
WITH PROTON. IF
FOUND, THE OTHERS
ARE NOT FAR AWAY.

NO CHARGE NEUTRON

Electrons and protons have a special feature called a
charge. Electrons have a negative charge, and protons
have a positive one. You've heard the saying, "opposites
attract?" Well, that especially applies to electrons. Their
negative charge is attracted to the positive protons. And
it's this attraction that makes electricity happen.

charge—a property of subatomic particles, such as protons and electrons

7

Take a Flying Leap

Atoms and all their parts don't stay in one place. They sort of vibrate around. As the atoms move, they come into contact with other atoms. Remember how electrons are attracted to protons? Well, if one atom comes near an atom with a stronger positive charge—Pouf! An electron from the first atom jumps to the positive one.

Here's another way to imagine it. Think of an atom as a merry-go-round. The merry-go-round's center is the nucleus. A few electrons calmly hold onto the seats as they spin around. The more reckless electron sits way at the edge. It just barely hangs on. As the merry-go-round spins faster and faster, the electron loses its hold. It flies off and lands on a passing atom.

We don't recommend trying this with a real merry-go-round. The landing would be shocking, but it wouldn't be from electricity.

When an atom loses an electron, it has a stronger positive charge than before. When it comes near another atom, it will attract a new electron. This movement of electrons creates electricity.

Chapter 2

Sock Shock and Wild Wire

Electricity can be divided into two types—static and current. Static electricity is the presence of an electric charge on a material's surface. The material gets a charge when it is rubbed with another material. Rub your stocking feet back and forth on the carpet. The rubbing causes electrons to bunch together, creating a negative charge. Then touch your finger to a metal object. Did you feel that jolt? That jolt was electrons flowing from your finger to the metal.

No, that doesn't mean electricity is divided into boring and cool groups. Both groups are equally awesome.

Lightning is also a form of static electricity. In this case, water molecules in clouds rub together. The rubbing causes a huge negative charge to build at the bottom of the cloud. Then … **CRACK!** The electrons shoot down to the positively charged ground, creating a lightning bolt.

Electrons always have such a negative influence.

You can also find static electricity in the dryer. The heat in the dryer doesn't just dry your clothes. It also moves electrons around. Some atoms might actually end up with too many electrons, giving the whole atom a negative charge. Atoms with too few electrons then have a positive charge. If you have positive atoms in your pants and negative atoms in your sock, what happens? They'll attract and stick together.

This may explain why there are so many missing socks. Although, we haven't ruled out leprechauns and aliens.

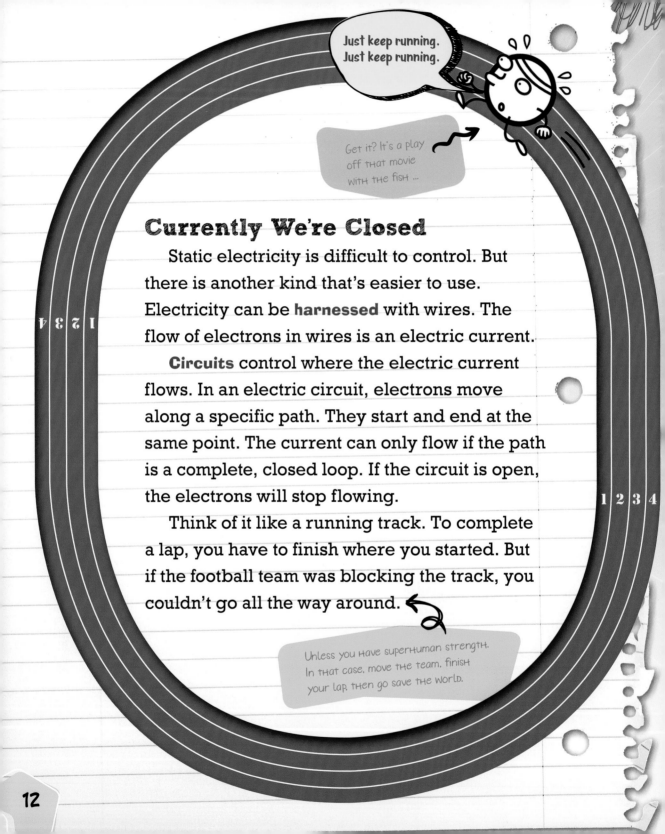

Just keep running. Just keep running.

Get it? It's a play off that movie with the fish ...

Currently We're Closed

Static electricity is difficult to control. But there is another kind that's easier to use. Electricity can be **harnessed** with wires. The flow of electrons in wires is an electric current.

Circuits control where the electric current flows. In an electric circuit, electrons move along a specific path. They start and end at the same point. The current can only flow if the path is a complete, closed loop. If the circuit is open, the electrons will stop flowing.

Think of it like a running track. To complete a lap, you have to finish where you started. But if the football team was blocking the track, you couldn't go all the way around.

Unless you have superhuman strength. In that case, move the team, finish your lap, then go save the world.

Electric circuits are all over your home. Just take a look at a lamp. Switch it on, and it lights up. Why? When you turn the switch, you close the circuit from the lamp to the outlet in the wall. Electrons then flow freely, creating electricity. The switch acts like a bridge. When the bridge is down, electrons move around the closed circuit. But turn the switch again, and the bridge lifts. This change leaves an opening in the circuit that electrons can't cross.

Don't keep switching the lights on and off, or your family will be cross with you.

Energy Source
Provides the "push" that makes current move around a circuit.

Load
Converts electrical energy to another form. In a lightbulb, it's turned to light and heat.

Wires
Connect the energy and load.

Switch
Opens and closes the circuit.

harness—to control and use something
circuit—the complete path of an electrical current

Conducting the Movement

Wires tie a circuit together. But the type of wire used in a circuit is very important. Certain materials allow electricity to flow more freely than others. These materials are called **conductors**.

Most conductors are metals. Metals have electrons that are less tightly bound to the nucleus. Remember the merry-go-round example? Metals have those electrons that are just waiting to jump off. Copper, aluminum, and iron are great examples of conductors.

If a band plays music during a thunderstorm, who is most likely to get struck by lightning?

Insulators are the exact opposite of conductors. They prevent electricity from flowing. An insulator keeps its electrons close and doesn't let them jump off.

To control electricity, insulators and conductors are used together. Take a look at the cord attached to your lamp. It's probably made of plastic. But inside the plastic are metal wires. The plastic on the outside keeps the electricity in place as it flows to the lightbulb. It also keeps you from getting a jolt. Without the plastic insulator, the electricity could travel to other objects, including you. The plastic keeps you from touching the wire that has electrons moving through it.

Insulators are like parents WHO ~~DON'T let you DO anything fun~~ keep you safe.

THe conDuctor!

conductor—material through which electric charges move easily
insulator—material that stops electricity from escaping

Hosing Things Down

So electrons fly as fast as they can through wires, right? Not exactly. Every wire has a type of **resistance**.

Resistance is a force that slows down the speed of electrons. Imagine the wire is a hose. The water flowing through the hose is electrons. When you turn on the hose, water flows freely. Now imagine some clumps of dirt have gotten inside the hose. That would make the water come out more slowly. The pieces of mud are a type of resistance.

The amount of resistance a wire has depends on the material it is made from. Copper has very little resistance. Electrons can flow really fast. But a wire made of iron or lead has a greater resistance. The electrons would move much slower down this type of wire.

I wonder HOW that could have happened ...

If they ever let you drive, you'll find that speed limits and cops are types of resistance too.

resistance—a force that opposes or slows the motion of something

Why does resistance matter? Resistance causes some electrical energy to turn into heat. If the **voltage** in a wire is too high, a lot of heat can build up. This buildup can cause a fire.

But it's this heat that makes lightbulbs work. The resistance in the bulb causes the **filaments** to glow. This glow lights our homes.

WHY DID THE LIGHTS GO OUT?

BECAUSE THEY LIKED EACH OTHER!

SORRY. WE TOLD YOU THE JOKES WOULDN'T GET ANY BETTER.

voltage—the force of an electrical current; voltage is measured in volts
filament—a thin wire that is heated electrically to produce light

Wired Ways

Circuits come in two types—series and parallel. In a series circuit, electricity travels in one big circular path. You can add as many toasters, TVs, or other **loads** to the circuit as you want. All the loads on a series circuit are connected with the same wire. So each load gets electricity in turn.

Series circuits have some downfalls. If a load in a series fails, the entire circuit shuts down. Think of the old Christmas lights you use each year. If one light goes out, the whole line of them goes out.

And Dad's patience goes out too.

Another problem with series circuits is that only one wire is used for all the loads. So a series circuit has a lot of resistance. Electrons slow down as they move along the wire. The load at the end of the series gets fewer electrons than the one at the start.

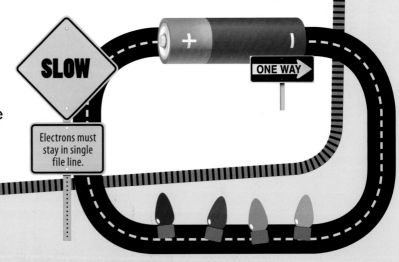

SLOW

Electrons must stay in single file line.

ONE WAY

load—a device to which power is delivered

In a parallel circuit, every load has its own wire. When the electrons see the different wires, they split up. Each wire gets the same amount of electrons. The advantage of this is that each lightbulb receives electricity at the same time. No waiting in line!

Also, the wires used in a parallel circuit are short. This type of circuit has less resistance.

It's almost as good as getting to cut in the lunch line on pizza day!

Most homes have parallel circuits. Parallel circuits do not fail as often as series circuits do. If one lightbulb burns out in a parallel circuit, the electricity still flows through the other paths.

SHARE THE LINE

Please move forward to the next available line.

19

Chapter 3

Getting the Power

Circuits are in everything from toy cars to monster trucks. But no matter where it is, electricity won't flow unless there's an energy source. Most of our gadgets get power from batteries. A battery stores energy in the form of a charge. One end of a battery has a positive charge. The other end has a negative charge.

The electrons at the negative end are packed very tightly. They are desperate for more elbow room! As soon as the circuit is closed, the electrons race through the wire. They rush to get to the positive side of the battery. Along the way, the electrons provide power to whatever load is attached to the circuit.

I imagine it's a lot like a big family reunion where you're squished between Grandma and Aunt Jean. You'd be negative too.

Batteries only contain so much charge. After you use them for awhile, the charge is spent. To keep the fun flowing, you'll need new, fully charged batteries.

 Doesn't it always seem like batteries run out of charge when you need them most?

 It might be a coincidence that it happens that way. But we can't rule out leprechauns and aliens here either.

Growing Electricity

Batteries power our cell phones, toys, and cars. But no one has a huge battery buried in their basement. So where does the electricity that powers our homes come from? It comes from a power plant.

This has nothing to do with flowers and bushes. We have no idea why both things are called plants.

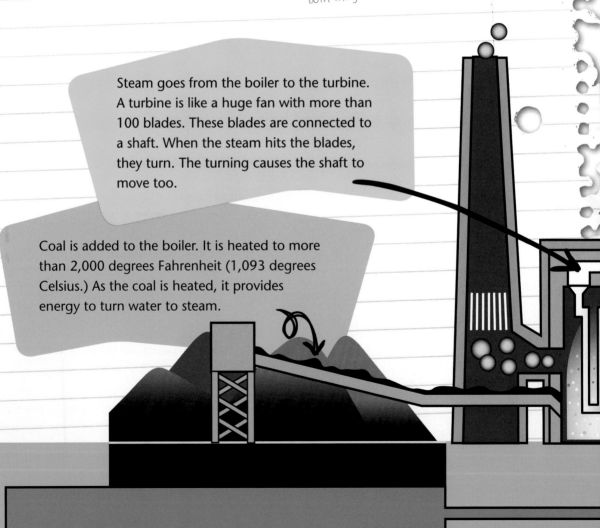

Steam goes from the boiler to the turbine. A turbine is like a huge fan with more than 100 blades. These blades are connected to a shaft. When the steam hits the blades, they turn. The turning causes the shaft to move too.

Coal is added to the boiler. It is heated to more than 2,000 degrees Fahrenheit (1,093 degrees Celsius.) As the coal is heated, it provides energy to turn water to steam.

Power plants use different materials to create electricity. Some burn coal, oil, or natural gas. Others use water, nuclear energy, or even heat from the Earth. Energy from these materials is then converted into electrical power. Here's how it works in a plant that uses coal.

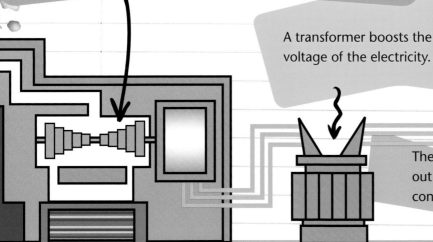

Large magnets wrapped in copper coil attach to the shaft. As the shaft rotates, the magnets spin and create a large **magnetic field** in the generator. The magnetic field creates movement of electrons. The electrons get so excited, they fly off and flow down a wire to a transformer.

A transformer boosts the voltage of the electricity.

The electricity is then sent out on power lines that connect to your home.

magnetic field—an area of moving electrical currents that affects other objects

Save the TV!

The power plant sends out electricity at about 400,000 volts. We mentioned voltage before. But what is it really? Voltage is how hard electricity is pushed through a wire. The power plant pushes a lot of electricity out. But compare that to most household appliances. They only need between 110 and 240 volts to run.

So why does the plant push so much electricity out? To get it to your home! At a high voltage, electricity can travel hundreds of miles without losing much charge. Electricity travels along the power lines until it reaches a smaller transformer closer to your house. This transformer "steps down" the voltage. It changes the voltage from 400,000 volts to a much lower voltage. Then the electricity travels through feeder lines right to your house. There, one final transformer makes sure the electricity is at just the right voltage.

We should have explained it on page 17, but we needed more room for that awesome joke about the lightbulbs.

I know you're waiting for a joke about those movie characters that change from trucks to awesome fighting machines. But those are copyrighted characters, so we can't use them.

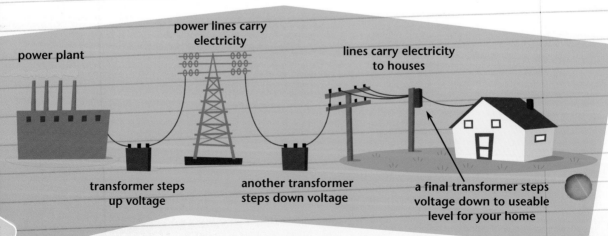

power plant

power lines carry electricity

lines carry electricity to houses

transformer steps up voltage

another transformer steps down voltage

a final transformer steps voltage down to useable level for your home

The process of "stepping down" the voltage is very important. Every appliance is built to run at a certain voltage. If it gets too much electricity, it could burn up. For example, most TVs are designed to work at about 110 volts. A higher voltage will make the TV burn more brightly and burn out much faster.

Home Improvement

Now you know how electricity gets to your house in the right voltage. But how does it get around the house? That's where circuits come in. Think back to the series and parallel circuit info. You have those in all of your walls. ←

Please don't rip out any walls to see them. Just look below at the nice picture we found. It's cheaper than repairing a wall.

The wires of each circuit go from the main power box in your house to an outlet and back. When you plug your TV into an outlet and turn it on, you complete the circuit. The electricity goes from the power box, through the wire, to the TV, and back to the power box. Then the only problem is choosing what to watch.

Finally some information you learn in school that you might actually use in real life!

See, isn't that a nice picture? Much nicer than a mess on the floor and a hole in the wall. You're welcome.

What Kind of Gas?

Electricity is a powerful force that is used all around the globe. But getting those electrons to rush around isn't easy. Many power plants are using coal, oil, and natural gas to make electricity. But those resources are nonrenewable, meaning they will run out.

Scientists are working to find ways to make electricity with renewable resources. Wind, water, and sunlight are just a few of the well-known alternatives. But researchers are investigating some new ideas too. Some countries are already using ocean tidal power. A few farmers are using gas captured from animal poop to light their barns.

Who knows what resources might help power our world in years to come? But one thing is sure. Electricity is a tiny turbocharged SUPERHERO that will continue to keep our planet lit.

WARNING: Do not read the next page immediately after eating. It may cause unexpected uprisings in your stomach area.

FART POWER!
Cows produce 211 to 264 gallons (800 to 1,000 liters) of gas each day. Some researchers have created back packs for the cows that catch that fart power. It might be possible to burn cow gas to power generators.

These are just a few of the more unusual alternative energy ideas. We didn't make this stuff up!

ROTTEN FOOD POWER!
One energy plant uses rotten food and cow poop to produce a burnable gas. Use this info next time Mom makes something gross for dinner. Thank her for making a renewable way to create electricity.

POOP POWER!
Each person on Earth pushes out about .5 pound (227 grams) of poop every day. Some water treatment facilities are using that flushed frenzy to make methane gas. Maybe someday your diarrhea will make electricity.

Glossary

charge (CHARJ)—a property of subatomic particles, such as protons and electrons, that can be positive or negative

circuit (SUHR-kuht)—the complete path of an electrical current

conductor (kuhn-DUHK-tuhr)—material through which electric charges move easily

filament (FI-luh-muhnt)—a thin wire that is heated electrically to produce light

harness (HAR-niss)—to control and use something

insulator (in-suh-LAY-tuhr)—material that blocks an electrical current

load (LOHD)—a device to which power is delivered

magnetic field (mag-NET-ic FEELD)—an area of moving electrical currents that affects other objects

resistance (ri-ZISS-tuhnss)—a force that opposes or slows the motion of something

voltage (VOHL-tij)—the force of an electrical current; voltage is measured in volts

Read More

Gangemi, Angelo. *Where Does Electricity Come From?* Everyday Mysteries. New York: Gareth Stevens Pub., 2012.

Oxlande, Chris. *Electricity.* How Does My Home Work? Chicago: Heinemann Library, 2013.

Stewart, Melissa. *Shockingly Silly Jokes about Electricity and Magnetism*. Super Silly Science Jokes. Berkeley Heights, N.J.: Enslow Publishers, 2013.

Woodford, Chris. *Electricity: Investigating the Presence and Flow of Electric Charge*. Scientific Pathways. New York: Rosen Central, 2013.

Internet Sites

FactHound offers a safe, fun way to find Internet sites related to this book. All of the sites on FactHound have been researched by our staff.

Here's all you do:

Visit *www.facthound.com*

Type in this code: 9781429686020

Check out projects, games and lots more at
www.capstonekids.com

Index

What is the smallest city? Electricity!